ABOUT THE AUTHOR

Neil Ardley has written a number of innovative nonfiction books for children, including *The Eyewitness Guide to Music.* He also worked closely with David Macaulay on *The Way Things Work.* In addition to being a well-known author in the fields of science, technology, and music, he is an accomplished musician who composes and performs both jazz and electronic music. He lives in Derbyshire, England, with his wife and daughter.

Project Editor Linda Martin
Art Editors Anita Ruddell and Peter Bailey
Photography Clive Streeter
Created by Dorling Kindersley Limited, London

Library of Congress Cataloging-in-Publication Data
Ardley, Neil.
The science book of water/by Neil Ardley.—1st U.S. ed.
p. cm.
"Gulliver books."
Summary: Simple experiments demonstrate the properties of water.
ISBN 0-15-200575-7
1. Water—Experiments—Juvenile literature. 2. Science—Experiments—Juvenile literature. 3. Light—Experiments—Juvenile literature. [1. Water—Experiments. 2. Experiments.]
I. Title.
Q164.A74 1991
532—dc20 90-37176
Printed in Belgium by Proost
First U.S. edition 1991
B C D E

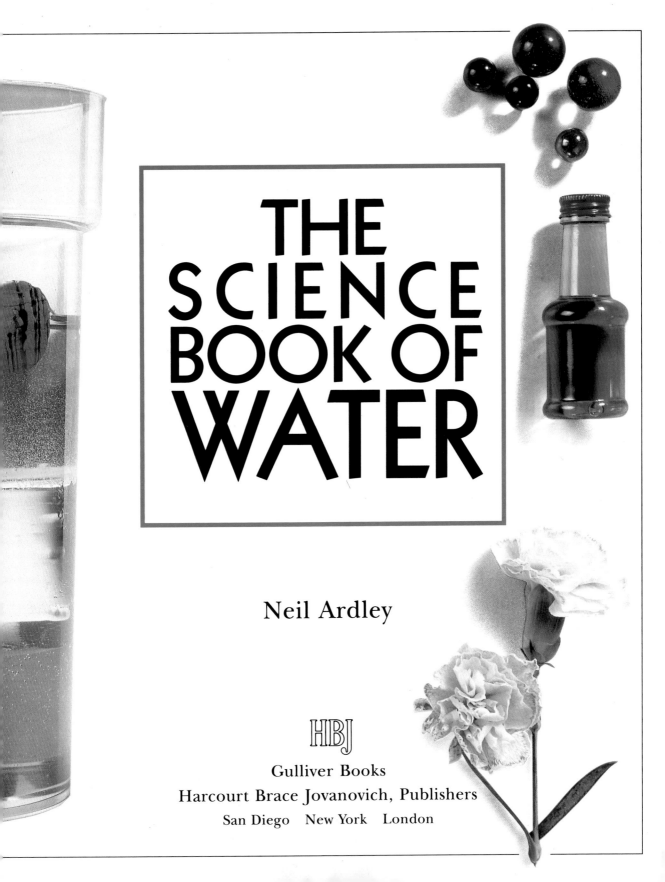

THE SCIENCE BOOK OF WATER

Neil Ardley

HBJ

Gulliver Books

Harcourt Brace Jovanovich, Publishers

San Diego   New York   London

What is water?

Water is not only fun to play with, it is also essential for life. All living things need water to survive. In fact, we can survive longer without food than without water to drink. Although we normally think of water as a liquid, it has two other forms. When it freezes solid, it becomes ice. When it is boiled, it becomes a gas called water vapor, which disappears into the air.

The power of water
Water can change the shape of land. The force of waves battering against the shore will eventually wear away the rocks, causing the cliffs to change their shape.

Mostly water
Did you know that more than half of your weight is the water in your body? The amount of water in these buckets is about the same as the amount of water in this girl's body.

Watery world
Water is almost everywhere. Oceans and seas cover nearly three-quarters of the earth's surface.

Snow play
When water vapor in the air freezes, it becomes ice or snow.

Wet weather
Water affects the weather. When there is too much water vapor in the air, clouds form and it rains.

⚠ This is a warning symbol. It appears within an experiment next to a step that requires caution. When you see this symbol, ask an adult for help.

Be a safe scientist
Follow all the instructions carefully and always use caution, especially with glass, scissors, matches, candles, and electricity. Never put anything into your mouth or eyes. You can make a mess with water, so remember to clean up and dry everything when you have finished the experiment.

Water weight lifter

Impress your friends with your strength! Ask them to lift a heavy bag of stones. They will find it difficult. But you can lift it easily–with the help of some water.

You will need:

Water

Stones

Large plastic bowl

Plastic shopping bag

1 Put the stones into the plastic bag. Ask a friend to lift the bag. It takes a lot of effort.

2 Take out the stones. Put the plastic bag into the bowl. Now fill the bag with the stones again.

3 Pour some water into the bowl. Be careful not to get any water in the bag.

4 Now lift the bag of stones. This time it is easier. The bag feels much lighter.

The water pushes up underneath the bag of stones. It supports the bag.

Water support
You feel less heavy in water because the water supports your body. This support allows people recovering from injury to move around more easily in water. They can exercise and play in the water.

Floating and sinking

Why do big, heavy things like ships float, but small objects sink in the water? It all depends on how much water an object pushes out of the way, or "displaces." Objects that displace lots of water receive a strong upward push from the water. This push can support the object so that it floats.

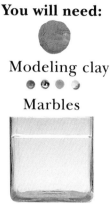

1 Drop the marbles into the water. They sink to the bottom. Now drop the ball of clay into the water.

2 The clay ball also sinks. Neither the marbles nor the ball pushes much water out of the way. This means there is not enough upward push from the water to support any of them.

3 Remove the marbles and clay from the water. Shape the clay into a boat.

4 Put the clay back into the water. Now it floats! The boat is larger than the ball, so it pushes more water out of the way. This means it receives a strong upward push from the water underneath.

The heavy boat gets more push from the water as it sinks lower—enough to keep it afloat.

Ships at sea
A large ship pushes a lot of water out of the way, so it gets a very strong upward push from the sea.

5 Add a "cargo" of marbles. The boat sinks lower in the water, but still floats.

Liquid levels

When you pour two liquids together, do they always mix? No. Certain liquids float or sink in other liquids. And do objects float or sink in liquids other than water? Test some liquids to find out.

You will need:

Tall, clear container

Grape

Water

Syrup

Cork

Plastic building block

Cooking oil

Oil is lighter, or less dense, than syrup.

Water is denser than oil, but less dense than syrup.

1 Pour the syrup into the container.

2 Pour in the same amount of oil. It floats on the syrup.

3 Now add the same amount of cold water. It sinks through the oil but floats on the syrup.

The cork floats on oil.

The plastic block sinks in oil but floats on water.

The grape sinks in oil and water but floats on syrup.

4 Put the cork, plastic block, and the grape in the container.

5 The objects float at different levels because they have different densities.

Oil at sea

Oil that spills from a tanker floats on the sea because the oil is lighter, or less dense, than sea water. Much of the oil is washed ashore by the incoming tide. This makes the beach very dirty, so it must be thoroughly cleaned.

Water volcano

Did you know that one kind of water can float on top of another? You can see this for yourself by making a "volcano" erupt under water.

You will need:

Glass tank or bowl

Water

Small bottle with cap

Ink or food coloring

1 Pour cold water into the tank until it is about three-quarters full.

2 ⚠ Fill the bottle with hot tap water. Add a few drops of ink or food coloring.

3 Screw the cap back on the bottle and shake it well.

Make sure the ink or food coloring is well mixed with the water.

Water becomes less dense when it is heated. This makes it lighter than cold water.

4 Place the bottle on the bottom of the tank and unscrew the cap.

5 The hot water from the bottle is lighter, or less "dense," than the cold water, so it shoots to the top of the tank.

6 The hot, colored water forms a layer on top of the cold water. As it cools, the colored water mixes with the cold water.

Hot-water holes
A column of hot water shoots up from a vent, or hole in the ocean floor, far below the surface.

Leaping water

Does water sometimes flow uphill? You can build a fountain and find out how to make water leap high in the air.

You will need:

Tape   Funnel

Pin

Plastic tubing

Water

Hold the sealed end of the tube above the funnel.

1 Push the funnel into one end of the plastic tube. Seal the other end tightly with tape. Make a small hole in the tape with the pin.

2 Pour enough water into the funnel to fill the tube.

3 Hold the tube over a sink and slightly lower the sealed end. Water begins to flow from the pinhole.

The weight of the water pushes it out of the tube and into the air.

4 Now lower the sealed end further. Water shoots from the hole, just like a fountain.

Fountain power
Water flows from a lake high in the hills to feed this fountain. Because the lake water is higher than the fountain, its weight pushes the fountain water into the air.

Deep-water diver

How do submarines dive and return to the surface? With just a few simple objects, you can make your own toy "diver." This diver will sink and rise in a bottle of water, in just the same way that a submarine dives and surfaces in the sea.

You will need:

Plastic pen top

Glass of water

Modeling clay

Thin, clear plastic bottle

If your pen top has a hole in the tip, seal it with a little modeling clay.

1 Stick a small piece of clay onto the pen top. This is the diver.

The diver should just float.

Air inside the pen top makes it float.

2 Put the diver into a glass of water. Remove or add modeling clay until the diver floats upright.

3 Completely fill the bottle with water. Put the diver in and screw the top on tightly.

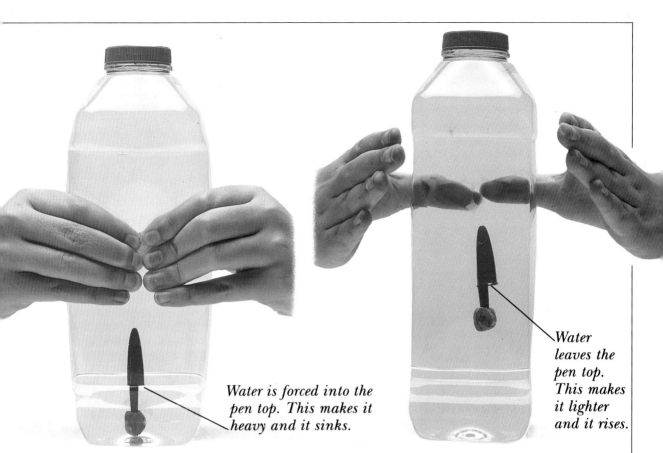

Water is forced into the pen top. This makes it heavy and it sinks.

Water leaves the pen top. This makes it lighter and it rises.

4 Squeeze the bottle very hard. The diver sinks to the bottom.

5 Let go of the bottle. Now the diver rises to the top again.

Underwater exploration

Submarines and underwater vessels that explore the ocean depths contain special tanks that are flooded with water to make them dive. Pumping air into the tanks to remove the water makes the vessels lighter, and they rise to the surface.

Speedboats

Make a boat that shoots forward when you touch the surface of the water behind it. This shows that water has a strong force on its surface, called "surface tension," that pulls at things floating on the water.

You will need:

Large, clean bowl of water

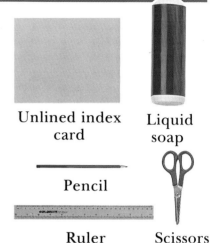

Unlined index card

Liquid soap

Pencil

Ruler

Scissors

1 Draw a simple boat shape on the index card.

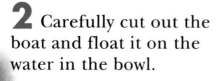

2 Carefully cut out the boat and float it on the water in the bowl.

3 Put a drop of liquid soap on your finger.

4 When the water is still, gently touch the water behind the boat with your finger. The boat shoots forward.

The liquid soap weakens the pull of the water's surface tension behind the boat.

The pull of the surface tension is stronger in front of the boat, so the boat is pulled forward.

Change the water in the bowl before you try again.

Washing dishes

Dish soap helps water to get dirty dishes clean. It weakens the grip with which dirt and grease stick to dishes. This makes it easier for the water to pull the dirt and grease off during washing.

Vanishing water

Do you know what happens to the water in wet clothes when they are hung up to dry? This simple experiment will show you how water disappears, or "evaporates," into thin air.

You will need:

Saucer
Water
Glass bowl

Pen

Small glass

1 Draw a line on the glass with the pen.

2 Pour water into the glass up to the line.

Take care not to spill any water.

3 Pour the water from the glass into the saucer.

4 Fill the glass with water to the line again.

5 Cover the glass with the bowl. Leave both the saucer and the covered glass in a warm place for several hours.

The water level does not fall. The water vapor cannot escape because it is trapped by the bowl.

Water evaporates more quickly when it is warm.

6 The water in the saucer eventually vanishes. Water that is open to the air forms water vapor, which is invisible. This vapor mixes with the air and is carried away.

Wet washing
When wet clothes are hung up to dry, the water changes into invisible water vapor that mixes with the air. Gradually all the water evaporates and the clothes become dry.

Water from nowhere

Why do drops of water appear on plants on cold mornings, even when it has not been raining? By cooling some air, you can show that the water comes out of thin air! This will also show you how clouds, mist, and fog form in the air.

You will need:

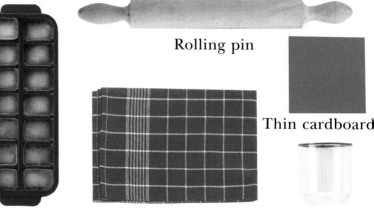

Rolling pin

Thin cardboard

Ice cubes

Towel

Glass

1 Wrap some ice cubes in the towel.

Press down firmly on the ice with the rolling pin. There is no need to bang it hard!

2 Crush the ice cubes with the rolling pin. You may need an adult to do this for you.

3 Make sure the glass is completely dry. Pour the crushed ice into it.

4 Cover the glass with the cardboard and wait for a few minutes.

5 The side of the glass becomes misty. Run a finger round the glass. It is wet.

The ice cools the glass and the air around it. Cold air cannot hold much water vapor, so some vapor changes into drops of water.

Tiny drops of water appear on the glass.

Early morning dew
On a cold morning, the air cannot hold much water vapor. Some of it changes into tiny drops of water, called dew, where the moist air meets the cold ground. Clouds, mist, and fog contain tiny drops of water that form and float in cold air.

Catch a cube

Challenge a friend to lift an ice cube with a piece of thread without tying a knot or touching the cube. It seems impossible, but you can do it easily.

You will need:

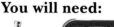

Salt   Ice cubes   Thick thread

1 Soak the thread in water and lay it on top of the ice cube.

2 Sprinkle a little salt all along the thread. Wait for about 30 seconds.

The salt makes some of the ice turn to water.

3 Lift the thread and up comes the ice cube!

The coldness of the ice freezes the water again, trapping the thread in the cube.

Safety in the snow
A snowy or icy road is dangerous because it is very slippery. Putting salt on the road turns the ice or snow to water, and makes the road safe for traffic.

Ice needs space

See how water grows, or "expands," when it freezes to ice. Nothing can stop it taking up more space. Ice can even burst metal pipes.

You will need

Water

Aluminum foil

Funnel

Small, thick glass or plastic bottle

1 Using the funnel and pitcher, completely fill the bottle with water.

Use a bottle with a narrow neck.

2 Cover the bottle *loosely* with foil. Put it in the freezer. Leave the water to freeze solid.

3 ⚠ As the ice forms, it pushes up the foil. Be careful, the glass may shatter.

There is not enough room in the bottle for all the ice, so some sticks out of the top.

Protecting pipes

In very cold weather, the water inside pipes may freeze. As it expands, ice can burst the pipe. Wrapping cloth around pipes helps to stop the water from freezing.

Funny flowers

By making plants change color, you can see how they obtain the water they need to live.

You will need:

Two fresh white flowers

Three glasses of water

Red, green, and blue food coloring

Celery with leaves

Scissors

1 Add a different food coloring to each glass of water.

2 Carefully split the stem of one flower to just under the flower head.

Trim the ends of each stem.

3 Put each half of the split-stemmed flower in a different glass. Put the flower with the whole stem in the other glass.

The whole stem feeds green water to all the petals of this flower.

This half of the stem feeds red water to the same half of the flower.

Blue water rises up this part of the stem to the other half of the flower.

4 Put the flowers in a warm room. After a few hours, they begin to change color. They draw the colored water up the stem to the petals.

5 Trim the end of a piece of celery and put it in a glass of red water. The water travels up the stalk to the leaves and they turn red.

If you cut across the celery, you can see the veins that carry the water to the leaves.

Picture credits

(Picture credits abbreviation key: B=below, C=center, L=left, R=right, T=top)

Brian Cosgrove: 7CR; Derbyshire Countryside Ltd/Andy Williams: 17BC; Pete Gardner: 6BC, 7TL; Malvin Van Gelderen: 23BL; Sally and Richard Greenhill: 9CL; The Image Bank: 6TR; NHPA/Manfred Danegger: 25BL; Science Photo Library/Adam Hart-Davis: 26BL; Ron Church: 19BL; M Fraudreau Rapho: 13BL; Peter Ryan/Scripps: 15BR; Spectrum Colour Library: 27BL; Zefa: 7TR, 11BR, 21BL

Picture research Kate Fox

Title page photography Dave King

Dorling Kindersley would like to thank Claire Gillard for editorial assistance and Mark Regardsoe for design assistance; Mrs Bradbury, the staff and children of Allfarthing Junior School, Wandsworth, especially Melanie Best; Nadia Agadia, Katie Martin, and Kate Whiteway.